Fozzie's Great Adoption Day Adventure

Bradley Kading

First Edition

Fulton Books
Meadville, PA

Published by Fulton Books 2023

ISBN 979-8-88731-624-6 (paperback)
ISBN 979-8-88982-001-7 (hardcover)
ISBN 979-8-88731-625-3 (digital)

Printed in the United States of America

To my wife, Kim, whose perseverance found Fozzie for us to adopt and love. She made both of our lives better. We made a family. You are much loved by adorable dogs and humans alike.

CONTENTS

PREFACE

When I was five, I was adopted from my foster home. I got scared and ran away. It was frightening; it was thrilling. The humans still talk and laugh about it to this day, but they get it mixed up sometimes, so I barked out this true adoption day story.

Fozzie

CHAPTER 1

A Change is Coming

It was all overwhelming. Lots of people would visit me weekly at the adoption center, but I was five, so kind of old for the puppy seekers. I knew the drill. I'd seen this happen several times after I was rescued off the streets in my old neighborhood where the bad people once kept me. The rescue people had cleaned me up, played ball with me, and fed me really well, so I was comfortable.

Then one day, these new humans came in, and the vibe was all different. Change was in the air. I could tell my foster parent and the doggie rescue project staff were suddenly serious. Papers were being signed. Treats spontaneously appeared to distract me, and then all of a sudden, I saw my leash and a pet-carrying case appear. In a flash, I was in a car with these new people.

After an hour ride, we drove up to a house in a place they called Washington, DC. The new guy put a combo leash/collar on over my head, and soon I was on the ground sniffing new territory. I knew I had never been here. Time for a walk.

BARKING!

CHAPTER 2

Scary Dogs and a Beautiful Ballroom Dancer

So far, so good. Lots of excellent smells on this new walk. By reading the pee mail, I could tell many dogs had been on this street. Soon we stopped in front of a nearby house where two dogs were playing in the small yard. Airedales—I'd seen their kind before, and I knew they were twice as big as me, kind of pushy and noisy. I was glad there was a fence between us. With them was a pretty, blonde-haired woman, kind of all dressed up. She was talking to the new guy. He told her (Katie Jane was her name) that they had adopted me. That's how I learned I was supposed to live nearby.

The two Airedales came right up to the fence and jumped at it trying to get closer to me. They were barking, and Katie was holding them back. They kept inching closer and closer, and I was afraid they'd jump right over the fence. I pulled back. The new guy kept a hold on my leash; Katie called him Brad. I kept inching back while the Airedales did their thing. My hairs were standing on end, but I knew my leash combination was loose and could slip over my head if I kept at it, so I did. I couldn't stand the noise anymore, so I gave one last backward push, and I was free. The leash and collar were off, and so was I. I took one last look at Brad, Katie, and her dogs and ran fast as I could down the sidewalk to the next street.

CHAPTER 3

The Great Race Begins

I turned around and saw two of them start to come after me. Katie was in a fancy dress and had heels on—dance shoes, I would later learn, for a ballroom dance program. It was a nice early spring day. I was ready for a sprint; I could tell they weren't. The Airedales were now nowhere to be seen. Their smells became faint. So this could be fun, I could play a race game with these humans. I would stop and turn around wagging my tail from time to time. I'd let them get closer, and then I would run as fast as I could, again feeling pretty good about my tease. I was now in the middle of Eighth Street running north. Lots of parked cars around me, so I couldn't see too well. That's why I stayed in the middle of the street, right on this painted line where my view was good. I could see people walking on the sidewalk pointing and laughing. They were enjoying my game. I looked back, and there were Brad and Katie running down the middle of the street after me. He was holding his own, but I could tell Katie was not keeping up with those heels and the fancy dance dress blowing up in the wind around her.

CHAPTER 4

The Firefighters Attempt a Capture

I kept running faster than they were. I was small and speedy, enjoying the breeze in my ears, but I noticed up ahead people were gathering. I could smell something; there was a faint smell of smoke. I knew this smell. Off to the side, there was a firetruck being washed and a fire station, stronger hints of smoke. I was attracting attention, but I didn't stop because Brad and Katie were weaving their way through the traffic following me.

Then I noticed other people in the street ahead. Three men in firefighter uniforms had spread out across the street in front of me. New players in my game. I sniffed them and stopped for a while. They were pointing and yelling at me. What were they doing? They moved toward me, but I dodged their hands, made a beeline between one guy's legs, and saw a clear path ahead of me. I barked out a laugh as I scored a run in my game.

CHAPTER 5

A Police Officer to the Rescue

I looked back, Katie was off to the side no longer in the chase, but Brad was there talking to a police officer on a bicycle. My hearing is excellent, so I heard part of the exchange.

"Is that your dog?" the officer said.

"Yes," Brad said panting, panting just like me.

"What's his name?"

"Uh, we just got him today, and we are naming him Fozzie, but he doesn't know his name. He was adopted. He got off the leash two blocks back."

"He doesn't know his name? Will he run home?"

"He doesn't know where his home is."

"Good grief. I'll follow the dog until we can corral him," the officer concluded.

I looked back, Brad was falling farther behind the bicycle officer, but the cop was on my tail, literally nearly on my tail! The game was about to change.

CHAPTER 6

The US Capitol Straight Ahead

More and more people were at the intersection and were looking and laughing at me and the cop and Brad all in a row down the middle of the street. So I turned left and jogged down the middle. Wonderful grass smells all around. I could see this big building a long way away at the end of the street. It was white, huge, and had a big dome on it. I heard the cop radio that I was headed toward the US Capitol Building straight ahead on Pennsylvania Avenue.

As I got near the intersection, I could see quite a commotion. Dozens of legs attached to nearly two dozen people now on both sides of the street, and two police cars were moving to block traffic at each side of Seventh Street. I knew police could be helpful, but what were they doing? I knew I was supposed to stop and look at what people called intersections. I could see that blocking traffic was going to make my run safer. Thank you, officers! So I put my chin down, my tail up, and speedily plowed forward. With my ears flowing in the breeze, I nodded and barked my thanks. I could see people clapping and cheering—for me of course. They liked my game.

CHAPTER 7

More Cops on Scooters Join My Game

I'd now been running about five blocks. I couldn't see the new guy, Brad, anymore, but two new police officers on scooters (called Segways) were now on either side of the bicycle cop. The crowds had thinned out, but I now had three cops following me. Were they going to play with me if I stopped? I didn't see or smell any treats, but now I was scared. Again, it had been an overwhelming day, and now it was three against one, and they were faster. The adoption, then the big intimidating Airedales, the fire fighters trying to grab me, and now these police officers on their scooters and bikes. I wanted it all to be over and be peaceful again, so I turned right onto a quieter Fourth Street to try to get away.

CHAPTER 8

The Wedding Party

I saw a big crowd on the left; it was a church. Beautiful music was wafting in the air. On the church steps, people gathered. Pretty soon, I saw lots of people in fancy clothes, the women in colorful gowns, and the men in black suits. The church doors opened, and I caught a glimpse of a young woman all dressed in white, carrying flowers. I didn't know what this was, but they started to point at me and my parade of bicycle and scooter cops. They all were laughing. At this point, I didn't want a crowd. All I wanted was a quiet place to lay down, some water to drink, and a cool breeze. Time to end this game in a safe place.

CHAPTER 9

The Open Gate and Shelter at Last

Now I was really tired. I had not run so much since that day long ago when I left the unsafe bad place. I had made a left turn onto East Capitol to try to shake my tail. Get it? The police were tailing me, my tail was shaking, but it was high and proud as I ran along. I woofed a greeting to another dog.

I noticed this street had broad front yards. I so wanted to stop and curl up in the cool grass, and then I saw my chance. There were fences all around, but in one area between two houses, there was an open gate. I made a quick right turn into the open gangway. At the end of it, there were some shrubs and a nice patch of grass. It smelled pleasantly of food, like garbage cans had been here. This reassured me. I stopped and I laid down in the shade. I was panting so hard my tongue was all the way out, and I was pooped. Even better, the three cops didn't follow me down the path. I noticed, though, they pulled up and closed the gate. They looked at me, and they didn't pursue me; they left me alone. I felt safe because I was fenced in. It was quiet; it was a cool, comfortable shady spot to rest. I had won the game. I dozed off.

CHAPTER 10

Dad's Back, Game Over

About thirty minutes later, I noticed one of the scooter police officers was back with the guy I now knew was Brad following him. He looked worn out and scared too. The cop pointed at me, and Brad strained to see down the path, trying to locate me among the shady bushes.

Pretty soon, he was talking to me, calling me Fozzie, saying he was so glad to find me again, that he'd been worried about me, that I would never feel unsafe again. He thanked the cop. They didn't pet each other, but they shook hands. He put the leash and collar over my head. He sat down on the sidewalk in front of me. He smelled different than the garbage smells, and for a while we panted together. I was thirsty, tired, and hungry. Soon, he lifted me into his arms; I needed that. He carried me out of the gangway. I was glad not to be running. I seemed safe. I felt protected. He held me in a tight hug that was reassuring. For the first time in what seemed ages, I was comfortable. Not another dog in smelling distance. Maybe this new guy would be okay.

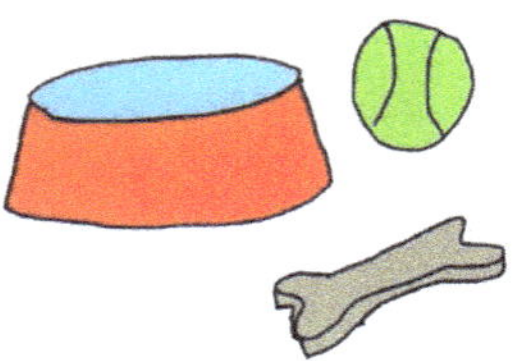

CHAPTER 11

The Reunion at My New Home

Brad walked and carried me more than a mile back to where I could remember the smells from when I had gotten out of the car, more than an hour ago. He didn't let go of me, and he never put me down on the ground even though I weighed more than twenty pounds. He seemed to not to want to let me go. I was okay with that and felt loved.

He opened the fence gate and carried me up the brick sidewalk of a narrow white house. I could see the front door was open. There was Katie, still in the heels and the fancy dress, and she was talking to the other woman who rode in the car with me earlier, after the adoption. I heard her name was Kim. Katie hugged Brad and petted me. She laughed and cried with joy about our return. Kim looked confused. Brad and Katie started to fill her in about my game. Hearing my adventure retold, it seemed overwhelming—the scary Airedales, the firefighters, the crowds cheering, the three police officers, the police cars safely blocking the busy intersection, the view of the Capitol, the wedding, and a sweet rest.

But here I was in what I now knew was my new home. I focused on the new smells. Kim gave me a bowl of water, some treats, and a new toy. I didn't have the energy to play, but I laid down with it and licked at it in between treats. I was safe. I had a new name and home, and I fell asleep.

EPILOGUE

This is my true story of my big adoption day adventure. The game had gotten out of hand. Luckily, it ended happily, and I adopted my new name, Fozzie, and lived with Brad and Kim for twelve more years. They loved me; I loved them. I loved my Capitol Hill daily walks and all the neighbor dogs (Woodruff, George, Rosie, Bobby, Talcum, Burger, Frederick, Hopper, and more). We made a happy family until one day, I could live no longer.

PS: My adoptive parents, Brad and Kim, later wrote their version of my true adventure story as a fond remembrance. No quibbles about it, but it doesn't have the pretty pictures that come with my version. Woof!

Fozzie

ABOUT THE AUTHOR

Brad and Kim Ross, both retired now, have lived in the same Washington, DC, Capitol Hill row house near the United States Marine Corps commandant's house and Barracks Row for more than thirty years. Brad's COVID project was documenting this true story. He retraced the route, and he consulted with Katie Jane (a longtime friend and dog lover) and the precinct police officers. Kim's brilliant suggestion was to turn this into a children's book.

In true Capitol Hill fashion, they've had two dogs to keep them company: Motown and Fozzie. Both were well-known neighborhood characters with many two and four-legged friends. Their longtime groomer, Valerie Johnson, kept them looking beautiful, and Doctor Dan Murphy and his team at the Capitol Hill Animal Clinic kept them both healthy. Capitol Hill's best pet store, Howl to the Chief, kept them supplied with their favorite toys and food. They are both gone, but not forgotten by the Capitol Hill community.

Special thanks to the District of Columbia Metropolitan Police Department, First District Substation. Their officers saved the day and beat Fozzie at his game. Also thanks to the firefighters of the District of Columbia Fire Department, Engine Company #18, Truck Company 7—it was a gallant try at the early save. To that wedding party at the Capitol Hill Presbyterian Church, you added a celebratory twist to Fozzie's game.

Special thanks also to Karen Laner and her young students at the Chiaravalle Montessori School in Evanston, Illinois, who, last year, gave approval to the book concept with their inspiring illustrations. Their early enthusiasm spurred me onto completion.

Special thanks to Christine Vineyard of Lidflutters.com, whose creative and fanciful illustrations make this story so much more appealing. She captured the spirit of Fozzie's adventure seemingly effortlessly. Her middle school students are lucky to have her as their art teacher.

Bradley Kading

CPSIA information can be obtained
at www.ICGtesting.com
Printed in the USA
JSHW042131270623
43832JS00007B/328